SANDY BEACHES OF AFRICA

A Journey Across Coastal Paradise

Sandy Beaches of Africa

1, Volume 1

LEONARD KISAU

Published by LEONARD KISAU, 2024.

SANDY BEACHES OF AFRICA

First edition. September 5, 2024.

ISBN: 979-8227956187

Written by LEONARD KISAU.

Also by LEONARD KISAU

1
Best Online Ventures in 2024
Raising Girls
Sandy Beaches of Africa
Cartoons & Me

Watch for more at https://www.familymedia.com.

To the breathtaking shores of Africa and the vibrant communities that call them home, this book is dedicated to you. To the fishermen, the travelers, the protectors of marine life, and the children who play in the sand—may your stories, traditions, and rich beauty continue to inspire and thrive. And to my daughters, who remind me daily of the wonder and magic found in the world around us, this is a tribute to the awe-inspiring nature that connects us all.

Introduction

Africa's coastline stretches over 18,950 miles, encompassing some of the most spectacular beaches in the world. From the golden sands of the Mediterranean to the untamed shores of the Atlantic and the warm waters of the Indian Ocean, African beaches offer an unparalleled blend of natural beauty, rich culture, and diverse ecosystems. These beaches are not just places for relaxation; they are vibrant hubs of life, where local communities thrive, age-old traditions are preserved, and nature's wonders unfold in every wave. In this eBook, we will explore the most captivating beaches across Africa, each with its own unique story to tell. Whether you are a seasoned traveler or someone dreaming of your next escape, this journey through Africa's beaches will ignite your wanderlust and deepen your appreciation for this extraordinary continent.

Africa is a land rich in diversity, culture, and natural beauty, with its beaches being some of the most stunning in the world. From the golden shores of Egypt to the pristine, turquoise waters of Seychelles, the African coastline offers a vibrant tapestry of sights, sounds, and experiences. African beaches aren't just about the sand and the sea—they're a blend of nature, history, culture, and adventure. Whether you're seeking relaxation, adventure, or a cultural journey, the beaches of Africa cater to every traveler's dream. The continent's coastline stretches over 30,000 kilometers, and within this vast area lies hidden gems waiting to be explored.

Take a trip to Zanzibar, a Tanzanian island paradise known for its spice trade and history as a major trading hub. The beaches of Zanzibar, such as Nungwi and Kendwa, boast soft white sands, warm waters, and stunning sunsets that leave a lasting impression on all who visit. As the tide recedes, locals can be seen gathering seaweed while dhows, traditional wooden boats, glide effortlessly over the horizon. Zanzibar's beauty is not just in its landscapes, but also in the rich cultural heritage that includes influences from Arab, Indian, and African traditions. It's easy to lose yourself in the history of Stone Town before making your way back to the beach for a relaxing day in the sun.

Cape Verde, a cluster of islands off the west coast of Africa, offers an entirely different experience with its volcanic landscapes and dramatic beaches. Sal Island, with its golden sands and aquamarine waters, is perfect for windsurfing and kitesurfing enthusiasts. The beaches here are a hotspot for water sports, and the consistent winds make it a favorite for thrill-seekers. However, life on Cape Verdean beaches is also about embracing the relaxed island culture. The rhythm of life is slow, and as you walk along the beach, you'll find fishermen returning from the sea with their daily catch, ready to be sold at the local markets. In the evening, the beaches come alive with the sound of Cape Verdean morna music.

For those seeking luxury, the beaches of Seychelles are unmatched. Known for their crystal-clear waters, powdery sands, and giant granite boulders, beaches like Anse Source d'Argent and Beau Vallon are consistently ranked among the world's best. The beauty of these beaches is surreal, with palm trees gently swaying in the breeze and the waters teeming with vibrant marine life. Diving and snorkeling in Seychelles offer the chance to encounter sea turtles, manta rays, and colorful coral reefs. The island's beaches are the perfect spot for honeymooners, offering seclusion and romance in one of the most beautiful settings imaginable.

In Egypt, the beaches along the Red Sea offer a fascinating blend of ancient history and modern luxury. Resorts like Sharm El Sheikh and Hurghada are famed for their vibrant coral reefs and clear waters, making them a haven for diving enthusiasts. The Red Sea is one of the most biologically diverse marine ecosystems in the world, offering encounters with dolphins, sharks, and even the occasional dugong. Away from the water, the sandy shores are a gateway to the country's rich history, with ancient temples and tombs just a short distance away. The juxtaposition of diving into crystal-clear waters and then exploring millennia-old pyramids is a unique experience only Egypt can offer.

Mauritius is another African gem, known for its coral reefs, lagoons, and breathtaking beaches. Grand Baie and Flic en Flac are among the most famous, drawing visitors with their pristine waters and opportunities for water sports, including deep-sea fishing and sailing. The beaches of Mauritius are also perfect for those seeking relaxation, with beachside massages and fresh seafood readily available. The local Creole culture, with its blend of African, French, Indian, and Chinese influences, adds a unique flavor to the island experience. As the sun sets, the beaches are often filled with the sound of sega music, a vibrant and rhythmic expression of Mauritian identity.

Mozambique's coastline, stretching over 2,500 kilometers, is home to some of the most untouched and unspoiled beaches in Africa. Tofo Beach, with its endless stretches of golden sand and vibrant marine life, is a haven for divers and surfers alike. The waters off Mozambique are home to one of the largest concentrations of whale sharks and manta rays in the world, making it a must-visit destination for marine enthusiasts. The local culture is equally captivating, with Portuguese influences seen in the architecture and cuisine. Seafood lovers will find no shortage of fresh prawns, crab, and fish, often grilled to perfection right on the beach.

For those wanting to explore West Africa, Ghana's beaches provide a unique blend of history, culture, and relaxation. Cape Coast, once a key hub in the transatlantic slave trade, is now a popular beach destination where visitors can reflect on history at the Cape Coast Castle before enjoying the serene beauty of the coast. The local fishing villages along the coast offer a glimpse into daily life, where fishermen cast their nets and women sell fresh produce in bustling markets. Labadi Beach, near the capital Accra, is a lively spot where locals and tourists alike gather to enjoy live music, dance, and local cuisine.

South Africa's beaches are just as diverse as the country itself. From the wild and rugged coastline of the Eastern Cape to the glamorous sands of Camps Bay in Cape Town, there's something for every type of beachgoer. The beaches along the Garden Route, such as Plettenberg

Bay and Knysna, are renowned for their scenic beauty and abundant wildlife. Dolphin and whale watching are popular activities, while the dramatic cliffs and lush forests make for unforgettable hikes. Meanwhile, the beaches of Durban offer warm waters and a laid-back vibe, perfect for surfing and family-friendly fun.

Namibia's Skeleton Coast offers a stark contrast to the typical tropical beach, with its windswept dunes, shipwrecks, and vast desert landscapes. It's a hauntingly beautiful stretch of coastline, where the desert meets the Atlantic Ocean in a dramatic display of nature's power. The Skeleton Coast is not a place for swimming or sunbathing, but for adventure and exploration. The beaches here are home to colonies of seals, and the skies are often filled with seabirds. It's a place that feels like the edge of the world, offering solitude and the chance to connect with nature in its rawest form.

Lastly, the beaches of Senegal, particularly those around Dakar and the Petite Côte, offer a rich cultural experience alongside the sun and sea. Ngor Beach, just a short boat ride from Dakar, is a favorite among surfers, while Saly offers a more relaxed atmosphere with its beachfront resorts. The vibrant culture of Senegal is evident on its beaches, where drumming, dancing, and local markets add to the lively atmosphere. The beaches are also a gateway to Senegal's famous hospitality, where visitors are welcomed with open arms and treated to the country's delicious cuisine, including fresh fish and spicy yassa chicken.

Africa's beaches are as diverse as the continent itself. Whether you're looking for adventure, relaxation, or a cultural experience, the coastline of Africa offers something for everyone. From the pristine waters of Seychelles to the dramatic dunes of Namibia, each beach tells a story of the people, history, and nature that define it. For those willing to explore, the beaches of Africa are a treasure trove of unforgettable experiences. So pack your bags, grab your sunscreen, and get ready to discover the beauty and magic of Africa's coastline, where every beach is a journey in itself.

Chapter 1: The Enigmatic Shores of Zanzibar

Zanzibar, an archipelago off the coast of Tanzania, is renowned for its pristine beaches, each offering a slice of paradise. The powdery white sands of Nungwi Beach contrast sharply with the turquoise waters of the Indian Ocean, creating a postcard-perfect scene. Here, the days are long and lazy, with the sun casting a golden hue over the waters as dhows, traditional sailing vessels, glide by. Life on Zanzibar's beaches is a fascinating mix of Swahili culture, vibrant marine life, and the lingering scent of spices that the island is famous for. Visitors can immerse themselves in local traditions, such as fishing with the locals or exploring the bustling markets of Stone Town. As the sun sets, the beach comes alive with music, dance, and the aroma of freshly grilled seafood, making it a haven for those seeking both relaxation and cultural immersion.

The Enigmatic Shores of Zanzibar are more than just a beach destination—they are a gateway to the rich history and vibrant culture of East Africa. At Paje Beach, the windswept shores provide the perfect conditions for kite surfers and adventurers, while the calm, shallow waters invite visitors to wade into the ocean and discover the colorful coral reefs beneath the surface. The coral reefs surrounding Zanzibar's coast teem with life, offering snorkelers and divers the chance to witness schools of fish, dolphins, and even sea turtles. Above the water, life moves at a slower pace, with the sound of waves gently lapping against the shore as the backdrop to the island's daily rhythm. The warm, tropical climate, combined with the hospitality of the Zanzibari people, makes this beach an irresistible destination for those seeking both adventure and tranquility.

Moving inland from the beaches, the vibrant history of Zanzibar unfolds in every corner of Stone Town, a UNESCO World Heritage site. The narrow streets of this ancient town lead visitors through a labyrinth of old, coral-stone buildings, each telling a story of the island's rich past as a center of trade and commerce. Once a hub for spice trading, the scent of cloves, cinnamon, and cardamom still lingers in the air, a testament to Zanzibar's historical significance in the global spice trade. A short walk from the town's bustling markets brings you back to the tranquility of the coast, where the blend of ancient culture and modern luxury offers a unique and unforgettable beach experience.

Zanzibar's beaches also serve as an ideal base for those looking to explore the nearby island of Mnemba. Known for its exclusivity, Mnemba Island offers some of the most luxurious beach experiences in Africa. The private island, surrounded by vibrant coral reefs, is a sanctuary for marine life and provides unparalleled diving opportunities. Here, visitors can swim alongside whale sharks, the gentle giants of the ocean, or simply relax on the beach in total seclusion. Mnemba's untouched beauty and commitment to conservation make it a haven for eco-conscious travelers seeking a high-end, environmentally friendly retreat.

Beyond the world-class beaches and luxury resorts, Zanzibar is also a cultural crossroads. The island's long history as a melting pot of African, Arab, Persian, and European influences is evident in its cuisine, architecture, and music. Beachfront restaurants offer a tantalizing array of dishes that reflect the island's diverse heritage, from freshly caught seafood to spiced curries and pilaf rice. The rhythmic sounds of taarab music fill the air, blending Swahili melodies with Arabic and Indian influences, and inviting locals and visitors alike to dance under the stars. Whether you are savoring a local dish, swaying to the music, or simply lounging on the sand, Zanzibar's beaches offer an experience that goes far beyond the typical sun-and-sand vacation.

Zanzibar's beaches also provide a window into the island's thriving local industries. The intertidal zones around Paje and Jambiani beaches are used by women from local villages to farm seaweed, a sustainable practice that supports both the environment and the local economy.

Visitors can witness this centuries-old tradition, where seaweed is harvested, dried, and exported for use in cosmetics and food products worldwide. These beaches are not only beautiful but also vital to the livelihoods of the local communities, making them a living example of how tourism, culture, and environmental sustainability can coexist harmoniously.

As you continue your journey along Zanzibar's coast, you'll find that each beach has its unique charm and allure. Kendwa Beach, located on the northwestern tip of the island, is famous for its calm waters and stunning sunsets. Unlike the eastern beaches, which are affected by the tides, Kendwa offers year- round swimming and water sports, making it a favorite among travelers seeking both relaxation and adventure. The nightlife here is vibrant, with beach parties and full moon celebrations adding an extra layer of excitement to the already dynamic atmosphere. It's a beach where the energy never wanes, and every evening feels like a celebration of life by the sea.

If you venture further south, you'll find the quiet beauty of Jambiani Beach. This stretch of coast is perfect for those looking to escape the crowds and immerse themselves in the slower pace of island life. Here, the traditional fishing villages remain untouched by mass tourism, offering visitors an authentic experience of daily life in Zanzibar. The beach is lined with palm trees, and the clear, shallow waters extend far into the horizon, making it a great spot for long walks and peaceful reflection. The simplicity of life on Jambiani Beach is its greatest charm, inviting you to slow down and appreciate the natural beauty that surrounds you.

Zanzibar's allure extends beyond its shores, with several nearby islands offering even more to explore. Prison Island, also known as Changuu Island, is a short boat ride from Stone Town and provides a glimpse into the island's colonial past. Originally built as a prison, it now serves as a sanctuary for giant Aldabra tortoises, some of which are over 150 years old. The island's clear waters and coral reefs are perfect for snorkeling, while its history adds an intriguing element to the day trip. Exploring the beaches and waters around Prison Island offers a unique combination of wildlife encounters and historical discovery, making it a must-visit for history buffs and nature lovers alike.

The biodiversity of Zanzibar's marine ecosystem is one of its most remarkable features. From the coral reefs that ring the island to the seagrass beds and mangroves that support a variety of marine species, the island's beaches are home to a rich and diverse array of wildlife. Conservation efforts are in place to protect these fragile ecosystems, ensuring that Zanzibar remains a haven for marine life. Visitors to the island are encouraged to participate in eco-friendly activities, such as snorkeling in designated areas, adopting sustainable travel practices, and supporting local conservation initiatives. The health of Zanzibar's beaches is deeply intertwined with the well-being of its environment, and protecting these ecosystems is crucial for the island's future.

Ultimately, what sets Zanzibar apart from other beach destinations is its ability to offer both cultural richness and natural beauty in equal measure. Whether you're exploring the labyrinthine streets of Stone Town, diving into the warm waters of the Indian Ocean, or simply relaxing on the sand, the island's beaches provide an experience that is as enriching as it is rejuvenating. Zanzibar's unique blend of history, culture, and natural wonder ensures that every visitor leaves with a deep appreciation for this magical island. With its pristine beaches, vibrant traditions, and commitment to sustainability, Zanzibar truly embodies the essence of an African coastal paradise.

Chapter 2: The Untamed Beauty of Namibia's Skeleton Coast

The Skeleton Coast, stretching along the northern part of Namibia's coastline, is one of the most remote and eerie beaches in Africa. Known for its treacherous waters and shipwrecks that dot the shore, this beach is where the desert meets the Atlantic Ocean in a dramatic display of nature's power. The landscape is hauntingly beautiful, with rolling sand dunes, rugged cliffs, and the remains of ancient ships telling tales of peril and survival. Despite its harsh environment, the Skeleton Coast is home to a surprising variety of wildlife, including seals, hyenas, and desert-adapted elephants. For the adventurous traveler, this beach offers a unique experience of solitude and awe, as you stand on the edge of the world where the desert kisses the sea. The Skeleton Coast is not just a beach; it's a reminder of nature's raw and untamed beauty, a place where you can truly feel the power of the elements.

The Skeleton Coast's desolate yet captivating beauty stems from its unique combination of desert and sea. The beach is named after the numerous shipwrecks and whale skeletons scattered along its shores, giving it an aura of mystery and danger. The region's unforgiving climate, with intense winds and thick fogs, has long been a challenge for sailors, leading to its reputation as a "graveyard of ships." Yet, for those willing to brave its stark landscape, the Skeleton Coast offers an unparalleled sense of adventure and exploration. The dunes rise and fall like waves frozen in time, and the ocean crashes against the shore with a relentless force, creating a soundscape that echoes the remoteness of this place.

Despite its harshness, the Skeleton Coast is teeming with life. The Cape Cross Seal Reserve, located along the coast, is home to one of the largest colonies of Cape fur seals in the world. Thousands of seals can be seen lounging on the rocks, their barks and calls filling the air as they navigate the cold waters of the Atlantic. Beyond the shore, desert-adapted lions, elephants, and hyenas roam the arid landscape in search of food, showcasing the incredible adaptability of wildlife in extreme environments. These animals have evolved to survive in conditions that seem impossible, a testament to the resilience of life even in the harshest of climates.

The allure of the Skeleton Coast lies not only in its natural beauty but also in its sense of isolation. For travelers seeking solitude, this is the ultimate destination. The vast, open spaces and minimal human presence make it feel like you've stepped into another world, far from the hustle and bustle of modern life. The beaches are often deserted, allowing visitors to take in the dramatic scenery in peace. As you walk along the shoreline, the sound of the waves crashing against the rocks and the eerie silence of the desert create a surreal experience that's difficult to find anywhere else.

Adventure seekers are drawn to the Skeleton Coast for more than just its beauty. The treacherous waters and unpredictable weather conditions make it a challenging destination for surfers and sailors alike. Those brave enough to navigate its waters are rewarded with some of the most exhilarating and unpredictable surfing conditions in the world. For hikers and off-road enthusiasts, the Skeleton Coast offers endless opportunities to explore its rugged terrain, from the towering dunes to the rocky cliffs that line the coast. The sense of accomplishment that comes from conquering such a harsh and unforgiving environment is unparalleled.

Cultural history is also an important part of the Skeleton Coast's appeal. The indigenous Himba people, who have lived in the region for centuries, continue to practice their traditional way of life, herding livestock and surviving in harmony with the desert. Visiting the Himba villages offers a glimpse into a culture that has remained largely untouched by modern influences. The Himba's intricate hairstyles, traditional clothing, and unique use of ochre to protect their skin from the harsh sun are fascinating aspects of their rich heritage. Engaging with the Himba people allows travelers to gain a deeper understanding of the challenges and rewards of living in such a remote part of the world.

The shipwrecks that litter the Skeleton Coast are a stark reminder of the dangers that once plagued sailors navigating these treacherous waters. Some of the wrecks are still visible, their rusting hulks half-buried in the sand, telling the stories of the perilous journeys that ended in disaster. Exploring these shipwrecks is like stepping back in time, offering a tangible connection to the history of the region. Each wreck has its own story, a testament to the power of the ocean and the unforgiving nature of the coast. For history buffs, the Skeleton Coast is a treasure trove of maritime lore.

In recent years, the Skeleton Coast has become a popular destination for eco-tourism, with a focus on preserving its fragile ecosystem. The Namib-Naukluft National Park, which encompasses much of the Skeleton Coast, is dedicated to the conservation of the unique flora and fauna that call the region home. Visitors can embark on guided eco-tours that emphasize responsible travel and sustainable practices, ensuring that this remote wilderness remains pristine for future generations. These tours often include visits to key conservation sites, where efforts to protect endangered species, such as the desert-adapted elephants, are in full swing.

The Skeleton Coast's appeal is also enhanced by its remote luxury lodges, which offer an opulent retreat in the heart of the wilderness. These eco-friendly lodges are designed to blend seamlessly with the natural surroundings, providing guests with stunning views of the desert and ocean. Despite the isolation, the lodges offer all the modern comforts, including gourmet meals, spa services, and private guides. Waking up to the sight of the sun rising over the dunes, with nothing but the vast desert and the sound of the ocean for company, is a truly unforgettable experience.

Photographers and artists are particularly drawn to the Skeleton Coast for its dramatic landscapes and unique light. The interplay between the desert and the ocean creates a palette of colors that changes throughout the day, from the deep blues of the Atlantic to the golden hues of the sand. The contrast between the jagged cliffs and the soft, rolling dunes provides endless inspiration for capturing the beauty and solitude of the coast. For artists seeking a muse, the Skeleton Coast offers a wealth of material to explore.

Namibia's Skeleton Coast stands as one of the most awe-inspiring and enigmatic beaches in Africa. It is a place where the raw beauty of nature is on full display, offering visitors a chance to connect with the elements and experience true solitude. Whether you're drawn to its wildlife, its cultural history, or its sheer sense of adventure, the Skeleton Coast is a destination that leaves a lasting impression on all who visit. It is a reminder of the untamed beauty of the natural world, a place where the desert meets the sea in a perfect, harmonious dance.

Chapter 3: The Vibrant Life of Dakar's Beaches

Dakar, the capital of Senegal, is famous for its lively and colorful beaches, where the rhythm of African life is palpable. Yoff Beach, one of Dakar's most popular spots, is a hive of activity from dawn till dusk. Fishermen bring in their daily catch, while children play soccer on the sand, and families gather for picnics. The beach is also a hub for local surfers, who ride the waves that the Atlantic generously provides. Dakar's beaches are not just about sun and sand; they are about community, culture, and the vibrant energy that defines Senegal. The sound of drums, the scent of grilled fish, and the laughter of people enjoying the simple pleasures of life make these beaches a sensory delight. For those looking to experience the heart of West African culture, Dakar's beaches offer an unforgettable immersion into the local way of life.

Dakar's beaches serve as cultural melting pots where locals and visitors alike gather to celebrate life, music, and the sea. Each day begins with the rhythmic hum of the waves crashing against the shore and the vibrant sight of fishermen preparing their pirogues—colorfully painted wooden boats—before heading out into the Atlantic. The local fishing trade is a deeply rooted tradition in Senegal, and Yoff Beach provides a glimpse into this age-old practice. As the sun rises higher in the sky, the beach transforms into a lively scene of people, with young and old alike coming together to work, play, and relax.

The vibrant markets that dot the coastline are a testament to Dakar's thriving beach economy. Vendors line the sands selling handmade crafts, colorful textiles, and delicious street food. Whether it's a plate of thieboudienne, Senegal's iconic rice and fish dish, or a refreshing sip of bissap, a hibiscus-based drink, the culinary offerings of Dakar's beaches are a feast for the senses. Street musicians add to the festive atmosphere, often playing traditional sabar drums, a sound synonymous with

Senegal's rich musical heritage. These musical performances often draw spontaneous crowds, turning the beach into an impromptu concert hall where locals and tourists share in the joy of rhythm and dance.

Beyond the food and music, Dakar's beaches play an important role in the spiritual life of the community. Along the shores of Yoff and Ngor Beach, it's not uncommon to see traditional healers offering blessings or spiritual cleansing ceremonies known as "ndeup." These practices are deeply connected to Senegal's religious and cultural beliefs, where the sea is revered as a powerful force that can heal, protect, and guide. The beach serves as both a sacred space for these rituals and a communal area where people seek spiritual balance through prayer and meditation.

Ngor Island, just off the coast of Dakar, is another popular beach destination that captures the essence of the city's coastal charm. Accessible by a short boat ride, Ngor Island offers a more tranquil experience compared to the bustling beaches of the mainland. The island's calm waters are perfect for swimming, snorkeling, and paddleboarding, while its sandy shores are ideal for sunbathing. Ngor is also home to several small restaurants and beach bars where visitors can enjoy fresh seafood, including grilled fish and oysters, caught just offshore. The island exudes a laid-back vibe that draws both locals and international tourists seeking a serene escape from the city's hustle.

For those looking for adventure, the beaches of Dakar are the starting point for thrilling water sports such as surfing, kitesurfing, and jet skiing. Yoff and Virage Beach are renowned for their consistent waves, attracting surfers from around the world. Dakar's surf culture is vibrant and inclusive, with local surf schools offering lessons for beginners and pros alike. The combination of warm waters, powerful swells, and a friendly surfing community makes Dakar an emerging destination in the global surfing scene. On weekends, Dakar's beaches become a focal point for families and groups of friends looking to enjoy a day by the sea. Senegalese families often bring homemade meals to the beach, setting up picnic spots where they can relax, eat, and socialize. It's not uncommon to see extended families gathered around large platters of food, sharing stories and laughter while enjoying the cool ocean breeze. This communal aspect of beach life in Dakar is one of its most endearing features—people are always eager to welcome newcomers, creating an atmosphere of warmth and hospitality.

In the evenings, as the sun sets over the Atlantic, Dakar's beaches take on a magical quality. The sky transforms into a palette of orange, pink, and purple hues, casting a soft glow over the sand and water. Beachfront cafes and restaurants light up, offering patrons a chance to dine with a view of the sunset. The scent of grilled seafood fills the air, and the sound of live music drifts from nearby venues, creating a perfect backdrop for an unforgettable evening.

For many, the beaches of Dakar represent more than just a place to relax—they are spaces where people come together to celebrate the Senegalese way of life. Whether it's through food, music, sport, or spirituality, Dakar's beaches offer a multifaceted experience that touches the heart and soul. The beach is a place where the past meets the present, where ancient traditions are honored alongside modern innovations, and where community ties are strengthened in the simplest of settings.

Dakar's beaches are also significant for their role in environmental preservation. Local NGOs and community groups often organize beach clean-up events to protect the coastline from pollution and to raise awareness about the importance of preserving marine ecosystems. These efforts reflect the city's growing commitment to sustainability, ensuring that future generations can continue to enjoy the natural beauty of Senegal's beaches.

As the tourism industry continues to grow in Dakar, the beaches are becoming a key attraction for international visitors. The city's strategic location as a gateway to West Africa makes it an accessible destination for travelers looking to experience the unique blend of African and European influences that define Senegal's culture. From backpackers seeking adventure to luxury tourists looking for a relaxing escape, Dakar's beaches offer something for everyone.

Overall, the vibrant life of Dakar's beaches is a celebration of Senegalese culture, community, and natural beauty. Whether you're exploring the bustling shores of Yoff or escaping to the tranquil waters of Ngor Island, the beaches of Dakar promise an experience that is both invigorating and enriching. For anyone looking to immerse themselves in the dynamic and welcoming spirit of West Africa, there's no better place to start than the beaches of Dakar.

Chapter 4: The Serenity of Anse Lazio in Seychelles

Anse Lazio, located on Praslin Island in Seychelles, is often hailed as one of the most beautiful beaches in the world. With its granite boulders, crystal-clear waters, and lush palm-fringed shores, Anse Lazio is the epitome of a tropical paradise. The beach is a sanctuary for those seeking peace and tranquility, far removed from the hustle and bustle of everyday life. The gentle waves lap at the shore, inviting visitors to take a dip in the warm, azure waters or simply relax on the soft sand. Snorkeling here is a dream, with a vibrant underwater world teeming with colorful fish and coral reefs. Anse Lazio is more than just a beach; it's a place where time seems to stand still, allowing you to reconnect with nature and find inner peace. The beauty of this beach lies not just in its physical appearance but in the sense of calm it bestows upon those who visit.

The magic of Anse Lazio unfolds as soon as you step foot onto its pristine shores. The soft, powdery sand feels like silk beneath your feet, and the rhythmic sound of waves crashing against the shore instantly lulls you into a state of relaxation. The towering granite boulders that flank both ends of the beach serve as silent guardians, framing the view of the endless turquoise horizon. It's no wonder that visitors often describe this beach as otherworldly, a hidden gem tucked away in the heart of the Indian Ocean. The gentle swaying of the palm trees and the occasional call of exotic birds complete the tranquil scene, making Anse Lazio a haven for those seeking solace in nature.

The water at Anse Lazio is an inviting shade of blue that seems to change with the light of the day. In the early morning, the water is a pale, shimmering blue, reflecting the soft hues of dawn. By midday, it deepens into a rich turquoise, while in the evening, it takes on a darker, more mysterious tone as the sun begins to set. For snorkelers and divers, Anse Lazio is a treasure trove of marine life. Just a few meters from the shore, the underwater world comes alive with schools of brightly colored fish darting among the coral reefs. Sea turtles glide gracefully through the water, their ancient forms a testament to the untouched beauty of this secluded spot.

One of the unique features of Anse Lazio is its sense of seclusion. Despite being one of the most popular beaches in Seychelles, it never feels crowded. The beach is long and wide, allowing everyone to find their own private corner to enjoy. Many visitors come to Anse Lazio not just for a day of sunbathing or swimming, but for the deep sense of peace that the place offers. It's a beach where you can lose yourself in a good book, take a leisurely stroll along the shore, or simply sit and watch the waves roll in, without a care in the world. There's a timeless quality to Anse Lazio that makes it feel like a world apart from the stresses of modern life.

As the day wears on, Anse Lazio takes on a new character. The heat of the midday sun gives way to the cooler, golden light of the late afternoon, casting long shadows on the sand. This is the perfect time to explore the boulders that line the beach, climbing them for a better view of the horizon. From the top, the view is breathtaking, with the entire beach laid out before you, framed by the lush, green hills of Praslin Island. As the sun begins to dip toward the horizon, the sky explodes in a riot of colors—pinks, purples, and oranges that reflect off the water, creating a picture-perfect moment that will stay with you long after you leave.

In the evening, Anse Lazio becomes even more magical. As the sun sets, the beach takes on a soft, ethereal glow. The temperature cools, and the sound of the waves becomes more pronounced in the quiet of the evening. Couples often stroll hand-in-hand along the shore, enjoying the romance of the setting. For those lucky enough to be staying in one of the nearby accommodations, a moonlit swim in the calm waters is the perfect way to end the day. The stars come out in full force, and the beach feels like a private retreat, far removed from the rest of the world.

The local wildlife also adds to the charm of Anse Lazio. During certain times of the year, giant tortoises can be spotted near the beach, slowly making their way through the underbrush. These gentle giants are native to the Seychelles and are a symbol of the islands' rich natural heritage. Birdwatchers will also find plenty to marvel at, with colorful tropical birds flitting through the trees and seabirds soaring above the ocean. The sounds of nature—the rustling of palm leaves, the distant calls of birds, and the gentle lapping of the waves—create a soothing soundtrack that accompanies your stay.

Beyond its natural beauty, Anse Lazio offers a glimpse into the local Seychellois culture. Though the beach itself remains largely undeveloped, there are a few small, family-run restaurants nearby where you can sample traditional Creole dishes made with fresh, local ingredients. Grilled fish, octopus curry, and tropical fruit are just a few of the delicacies on offer. Dining on the beach, with the sand between your toes and the ocean as your backdrop, is an experience like no other. The warm hospitality of the locals only adds to the charm of the place, making you feel like you are part of their island community, even if only for a short while.

For those seeking adventure, Anse Lazio offers plenty of opportunities to explore. Hiking trails wind through the surrounding hills, offering panoramic views of the beach and the surrounding islands. Kayaking and paddleboarding are also popular activities, allowing visitors to get a closer look at the crystal-clear waters and the diverse marine life that calls it home. Whether you're gliding across the water or hiking through the lush forests, the beauty of Anse Lazio is ever-present, reminding you at every turn of the island's unspoiled natural splendor.

While Anse Lazio is undoubtedly a place for relaxation and reflection, it is also a place of renewal. Many visitors leave the beach feeling rejuvenated, as if they have found a small piece of paradise that has somehow escaped the passage of time. The combination of the pristine environment, the calming atmosphere, and the gentle rhythm of life on the island creates a powerful sense of well-being. It's no wonder that Anse Lazio is often described as one of the most beautiful beaches in the world—it offers not just physical beauty, but a deeper connection to nature that is increasingly rare in today's fast- paced world.

As night falls on Anse Lazio, the beach takes on a new kind of beauty. The stars shine brightly overhead, and the sound of the waves becomes even more soothing in the stillness of the night. For those who stay late, the experience of sitting on the beach under the stars, with nothing but the sound of the ocean and the occasional rustle of palm leaves, is a memory that will last a lifetime. It's moments like these that make Anse Lazio more than just a beach—it's a place where you can truly disconnect from the outside world and find peace in the simplicity of nature.

In the end, the magic of Anse Lazio lies not just in its physical beauty, but in the way it makes you feel. It's a place where you can slow down, breathe deeply, and appreciate the natural world in all its glory. Whether you come for the snorkeling, the sunsets, or simply the serenity, Anse Lazio offers an experience that is both unforgettable and transformative. It's a reminder that, in a world full of noise and distractions, there are still places where you can find peace, quiet, and a deep connection to nature.

Chapter 5: The Hidden Gems of Mozambique's Quirimbas Archipelago

The Quirimbas Archipelago, located off the northern coast of Mozambique, is a collection of 32 coral islands that offer some of Africa's most pristine and unspoiled beaches. These islands are a hidden paradise, where powdery white sands meet the deep blue of the Indian Ocean, and time seems to move at its own leisurely pace. The beaches here are often deserted, offering a sense of exclusivity and serenity that is hard to find elsewhere. Life on these islands is simple and slow, with the local communities living in harmony with the natural environment. The Quirimbas Archipelago is a haven for marine life, making it a top destination for diving and snorkeling enthusiasts. The underwater world is vibrant and teeming with life, from colorful corals to schools of tropical fish and even the occasional sighting of dolphins and whales. The beauty of the Quirimbas lies in its untouched nature, offering a true escape from the modern world.

The Quirimbas Archipelago feels like a dream, a place where the modern world fades away and nature takes center stage. Each island in the chain has its own unique charm, but what they all share is a sense of untouched beauty. The beaches are lined with swaying palm trees, and the soft white sand stretches as far as the eye can see. You can walk for miles along the shore without encountering another soul, the only sounds being the gentle lapping of the waves and the occasional call of a seabird. The air here is warm and fragrant, carrying the scent of saltwater mixed with tropical blooms, creating a perfect backdrop for quiet contemplation or adventurous exploration.

In the early mornings, the islands come alive with the subtle hum of village life. Local fishermen set out in their traditional dhow boats, their sails billowing in the gentle breeze as they head out to sea. These boats, made from wood and sails of canvas, have been used for centuries, and watching them glide across the water is like stepping back in time. The fishermen return later in the day with their catch, a bounty of fresh fish, crabs, and lobsters that are sold in local markets or grilled right on the beach. This daily rhythm of life continues, unchanged for generations, giving visitors a glimpse into the simplicity and beauty of island living.

For those who love the ocean, the Quirimbas Archipelago offers a world of discovery beneath the waves. The coral reefs that surround the islands are some of the most well-preserved in the world, teeming with marine life that dazzles the senses. Snorkelers can drift along the surface, gazing down at the colorful fish darting between corals, while divers can descend into deeper waters where sea turtles, manta rays, and even sharks can be seen. The visibility is incredible, allowing for clear views of the underwater landscape, which seems almost too vibrant and alive to be real. It's not uncommon to come across pods of dolphins swimming nearby, their playful energy contagious as they leap out of the water.

One of the most magical experiences in the Quirimbas Archipelago is watching the sunset. As the sun dips toward the horizon, the sky is painted in shades of pink, orange, and purple, casting a warm glow over the islands. The reflection of the sunset on the calm waters creates a mirror effect, making it difficult to tell where the sea ends, and the sky begins. As darkness falls, the stars emerge in full force, twinkling above in a display that is rarely seen in light-polluted cities. It's the perfect setting for an evening walk along the beach, with the cool sand between your toes and the sound of the ocean as your only companion.

The islands also offer a rich cultural experience, with local communities that are eager to share their traditions and stories. The people of the Quirimbas are warm and welcoming, their lives deeply connected to the ocean and the land. Visitors can explore small villages where life moves at a different pace, and modern conveniences are few and far between. Here, it's easy to see how the locals have adapted to their environment, relying on fishing and small-scale farming to sustain their way of life. Craftsmen can be seen working on intricate carvings or weaving baskets from palm leaves, and the local women often sell handmade jewelry and textiles, adding a splash of color to the sandy streets.

For those seeking adventure, the Quirimbas Archipelago is a playground of natural wonders. From hiking through dense mangrove forests to kayaking along the winding waterways that cut through the islands, there is no shortage of ways to explore. The islands are also home to a variety of wildlife, including rare bird species, small mammals, and even the elusive dugong, a gentle marine mammal that is closely related to the manatee. Spotting one of these creatures is a rare and special moment, adding to the sense that the Quirimbas is a place where nature still reigns supreme.

The remoteness of the Quirimbas Archipelago is part of its appeal. Getting there requires a bit of effort, but for those who make the journey, the rewards are endless. The islands remain largely undeveloped, with only a handful of eco-friendly lodges and boutique hotels offering accommodation. These resorts are designed to blend into the natural landscape, ensuring that the islands retain their wild, untouched beauty. Guests are encouraged to disconnect from technology and reconnect with nature, spending their days exploring, relaxing, and soaking in the serenity of island life.

Despite its remote location, the Quirimbas Archipelago offers a range of luxurious experiences for those who seek them. From private beach picnics to sunset dhow cruises, the islands cater to those looking for an intimate and personalized escape. Many of the lodges offer spa treatments using natural ingredients sourced from the islands, adding an extra layer of indulgence to the experience. There's nothing quite like a massage with the sound of the ocean in the background, or a candlelit dinner on the beach with nothing but the stars overhead.

The history of the Quirimbas Archipelago is as rich as its natural beauty. The islands were once an important stop along the ancient spice and ivory trade routes, and remnants of this past can still be seen today. The island of Ibo, in particular, is a living museum, with its old forts, colonial buildings, and crumbling ruins offering a glimpse into a time when the islands were bustling with traders from Africa, the Middle East, and Europe. Walking through the narrow streets of Ibo, it's easy to imagine what life was like centuries ago, and the island's slow pace of life makes it feel as though time has stood still.

While the Quirimbas Archipelago is often considered a paradise for honeymooners and those seeking peace and solitude, it also offers plenty of activities for families. The calm, shallow waters are perfect for children to swim and play in, and the sense of adventure that comes with exploring the islands makes it an ideal destination for families looking to reconnect with nature. Whether it's building sandcastles on the beach, snorkeling together in the clear waters, or going on a guided nature walk to spot wildlife, there are endless opportunities for family fun and bonding.

One of the most remarkable things about the Quirimbas Archipelago is its commitment to conservation. Efforts are being made to protect the fragile ecosystems of the islands, with marine conservation projects aimed at preserving the coral reefs and the species that depend on them. Local communities are also involved in these efforts, recognizing the importance of sustainable tourism and fishing practices to ensure that future generations can continue to enjoy the islands' beauty. Visitors are encouraged to respect the environment, with many lodges offering eco-friendly tours and experiences that allow guests to learn more about the islands' delicate balance of nature.

The food in the Quirimbas Archipelago is another highlight, with fresh seafood being the star of the menu. Fish, lobster, crab, and prawns are caught daily and prepared in a variety of ways, from simple grilled dishes to more elaborate Creole-inspired recipes. The flavors are bold and vibrant, with influences from Africa, Portugal, and the Middle East all coming together to create a unique culinary experience. Dining on the beach, with the sound of the waves and the cool sea breeze, adds to the sensory delight, making every meal a memorable one.

In the end, the Quirimbas Archipelago is more than just a collection of beautiful islands; it's a place where the soul finds peace, and the mind can truly relax. Whether you're seeking adventure, romance, or simply a quiet escape from the world, the Quirimbas offers something for everyone. It's a place where the natural beauty is matched only by the warmth of the people, and where every moment feels like a gift. For those lucky enough to visit, the Quirimbas Archipelago leaves a lasting impression, a memory of a place where the land meets the sea in perfect harmony.

Chapter 6: The Cultural Richness of Cape Coast, Ghana

Cape Coast, located along Ghana's Atlantic coastline, is not just known for its beautiful beaches but also for its rich history and cultural significance. The sandy shores of Cape Coast are lined with historical landmarks, including the Cape Coast Castle, a UNESCO World Heritage Site that played a crucial role in the transatlantic slave trade. The beaches here are a blend of natural beauty and poignant history, offering a unique experience for visitors. The waves of the Atlantic Ocean crash against the shore, creating a powerful and mesmerizing backdrop to the area's deep historical narratives. Life on the beach is vibrant, with fishermen casting their nets, children playing, and the occasional cultural event bringing the community together. Cape Coast's beaches are a testament to the resilience and strength of the Ghanaian people, offering visitors a chance to reflect on history while enjoying the natural beauty of the coastline.

The story of Cape Coast begins with its stunning natural beauty, but it is deeply intertwined with a past that carries both sorrow and strength. The beaches, with their soft golden sands, stretch out along the Atlantic, kissed by the waves that once carried ships filled with people taken from their homes. Cape Coast Castle, perched on the edge of the beach, stands as a haunting reminder of the transatlantic slave trade. The castle's whitewashed walls hide a dark history, one that draws visitors seeking to understand the deep scars left by centuries of oppression. Walking along the beach, it's impossible not to feel the weight of history, yet the vibrant energy of the people here speaks of resilience and hope.

The local fishing community adds a unique dynamic to the atmosphere of Cape Coast's beaches. Each morning, before the sun rises, fishermen prepare their boats, ready to venture into the vast Atlantic Ocean. The sight of colorful canoes dotting the horizon is a common one, and the beach comes alive with activity as the catch is hauled in. The camaraderie among the fishermen is palpable as they work together, their strong hands pulling in nets filled with fish, crab, and lobster. For many visitors, joining these fishermen on their morning expeditions offers a rare glimpse into the daily lives of Cape Coast's coastal communities. It's a tradition that has been passed down through generations, connecting the people to the ocean and to each other.

Cultural festivals are a vibrant part of life in Cape Coast, and the beach often serves as the venue for these lively celebrations. The Fetu Afahye festival, held annually, is one such event where the entire community gathers to give thanks for a bountiful harvest and to honor their ancestors. The sound of drums fills the air, and traditional dancers, dressed in brightly colored attire, move in rhythm with the music. The beach becomes a stage for this cultural spectacle, where locals and visitors alike are invited to participate in the festivities. These events offer a glimpse into the rich cultural heritage of Ghana and provide a perfect balance to the solemn history associated with Cape Coast.

Exploring the coastline of Cape Coast is not just about history and culture; it's also about embracing the natural beauty that surrounds it. The coastline is dotted with secluded coves and hidden beaches, each offering a quiet retreat from the bustling town. These pockets of tranquility are perfect for swimming, sunbathing, or simply relaxing under the shade of a palm tree. The warm waters of the Atlantic invite visitors to take a refreshing dip, and the gentle waves provide the ideal setting for those looking to surf or paddleboard. Despite its historical significance, the beaches of Cape Coast remain a place of peace and relaxation, where the natural world seems untouched by time.

One of the most striking things about Cape Coast is how seamlessly history and everyday life coexist. The locals go about their daily routines, unfazed by the significance of the landmarks that surround them. For many, the beach is simply a place to work, play, and gather as a community. Children run along the shore, laughing as they chase each other through the sand, their voices mingling with the sound of the ocean. Vendors set up small stalls selling everything from fresh fruit to handmade crafts, and the smell of grilled fish fills the air. It's a scene of everyday life that contrasts sharply with the somber history of the nearby castle, yet both are essential to the identity of Cape Coast.

The sunsets in Cape Coast are nothing short of magical. As the day comes to an end, the sky is painted in hues of orange, pink, and purple, casting a golden glow over the beach. The silhouette of the Cape Coast Castle against the setting sun is a sight to behold, a moment where the beauty of the present meets the gravity of the past. Couples stroll hand in hand along the shore, while families gather to watch the day fade into night. It's a time for reflection, for remembering the past while appreciating the present, and for looking forward to the future with hope and determination.

At night, the beaches of Cape Coast take on a different energy. The sound of the waves becomes a soothing lullaby, and the beach is lit by the soft glow of lanterns from nearby homes and beachside eateries. It's a time for storytelling, a tradition that is deeply embedded in Ghanaian culture. Elders gather with children around small fires, sharing tales of bravery, wisdom, and the spirits of their ancestors. For visitors, these stories offer a deeper understanding of the people and their connection to the land, the sea, and their history. The night sky, dotted with stars, feels vast and endless, much like the stories that have been passed down through generations.

Cape Coast's beaches are also a gateway to exploration. Many visitors use the town as a base to explore the surrounding region, including Kakum National Park with its famous canopy walk, or the nearby town of Elmina, home to another significant slave castle. Day trips from Cape Coast offer the chance to experience Ghana's rich biodiversity and its role in the transatlantic slave trade. The contrast between the natural beauty of the rainforest and the weight of history in the castles provides a fuller picture of the region's complexities. Cape Coast's location makes it an ideal starting point for those looking to delve deeper into Ghana's history and landscapes.

Despite its painful past, Cape Coast is a town filled with hope for the future. The people here have turned their history into a source of strength, using it to educate and inspire change. The local community has embraced tourism as a way to share their story with the world, ensuring that the lessons of the past are never forgotten. Visitors leave Cape Coast with more than just memories of beautiful beaches; they leave with a deeper understanding of the resilience and spirit of the Ghanaian people. It's a place where history is not just remembered but lived, where the past informs the present, and where every grain of sand holds a story waiting to be told.

The local artisans of Cape Coast are a testament to the creativity and talent that thrives in this community. Along the beach, small shops and stalls display handmade crafts, from intricately woven baskets to vibrant paintings and jewelry. These items are more than just souvenirs; they are a reflection of the rich cultural heritage of the region. Many of the artisans incorporate traditional symbols and techniques into their work, preserving their craft for future generations. Visitors are encouraged to support these local businesses, not only as a way to take a piece of Cape Coast home with them but also to contribute to the sustainability of the community.

Cape Coast is also a place of education. The University of Cape Coast, located just a short distance from the beach, is one of the leading educational institutions in Ghana. The university attracts students from all over the country and beyond, adding to the vibrancy of the town. The presence of the university has fostered a culture of learning and intellectual curiosity in Cape Coast, and many visitors find themselves drawn into discussions with locals about history, politics, and the future of Ghana. It's a town where knowledge is valued, and where the lessons of the past are used to shape a better future.

Ultimately, the beauty of Cape Coast lies in its ability to hold both joy and sorrow, past and present, all at once. The beaches are a place of reflection, where the ocean's rhythm can bring a sense of peace and healing. At the same time, they are a place of life and laughter, where children play, families gather, and the future feels full of possibility. For those who visit, Cape Coast offers more than just a beach vacation. It offers a journey into the heart of Ghana, where the stories of the past are always present, and where every wave that crashes against the shore carries with it a reminder of the strength and resilience of the human spirit.

Chapter 7: The Luxury of Mauritius' Belle Mare Beach

Belle Mare Beach, located on the eastern coast of Mauritius, is synonymous with luxury and indulgence. This beach is renowned for its long stretch of powdery white sand, clear turquoise waters, and world-class resorts that cater to the most discerning travelers. Belle Mare is the perfect destination for those seeking relaxation and pampering in a stunning tropical setting. The beach offers a range of activities, from water sports like windsurfing and snorkeling to leisurely strolls along the shore at sunset. The gentle breeze, the sound of the waves, and the lush greenery that surrounds the beach create an atmosphere of tranquility and bliss. Visitors can indulge in spa treatments, gourmet dining, and private beach picnics, making Belle Mare a haven for those seeking the ultimate beach getaway. The luxury of Belle Mare Beach is not just in its amenities but in the overall experience of being enveloped in nature's beauty while enjoying the finest comforts.

Belle Mare Beach, with its pristine beauty and sophisticated charm, is a jewel on the east coast of Mauritius. The beach stretches for miles, offering soft, powdery white sand that feels like silk underfoot, while the crystal-clear turquoise waters beckon visitors for a refreshing dip. As you walk along the shore, the gentle breeze from the Indian Ocean caresses your skin, and the sound of the waves creates a serene soundtrack for your day. The lush greenery that frames the beach enhances its allure, making it a place where nature and luxury exist in perfect harmony. The sunrises at Belle Mare are particularly breathtaking, with hues of pink, orange, and gold painting the sky, a sight that sets the tone for a peaceful and indulgent day ahead.

For those seeking adventure, Belle Mare offers a plethora of water sports and activities. The calm, shallow waters are perfect for snorkeling, where you can explore vibrant coral reefs teeming with marine life just offshore. Windsurfing and paddleboarding are also popular choices, with the constant yet gentle breeze providing ideal conditions for gliding across the water. Deep-sea fishing excursions allow guests to venture out into the open ocean, where they can try their hand at catching exotic fish species. For visitors looking to explore the area further, luxury yachts are available for private charters, offering the opportunity to sail along the coast, taking in the island's stunning scenery from the water.

As the day progresses, the beach transforms into a place of indulgence and relaxation. Many of the world-class resorts that line Belle Mare Beach offer exclusive spa services, where visitors can enjoy treatments inspired by local ingredients such as coconut oil and sugarcane. These wellness sanctuaries provide a tranquil escape, allowing guests to rejuvenate their bodies and minds while overlooking the azure ocean. Private beach cabanas offer the perfect retreat for those wanting to enjoy the peace and beauty of Belle Mare in solitude. Here, you can sip on a cocktail or enjoy a fresh fruit platter, all while basking in the sun's warmth and listening to the rhythmic sound of the waves.

Dining at Belle Mare is an experience in itself, with many luxury resorts boasting award-winning restaurants that serve gourmet dishes crafted from the freshest local ingredients. The cuisine is a fusion of Creole, French, Indian, and Chinese influences, reflecting Mauritius' rich cultural heritage. Whether you're enjoying a casual beachfront barbecue or a multi-course fine dining experience, the food is always a highlight of any stay. Private dinners on the beach, complete with candlelight and personalized service, add a touch of romance to any vacation. As the sun sets and the stars begin to twinkle above, Belle Mare's dining venues come alive with soft music, laughter, and the clinking of glasses, creating an unforgettable evening ambiance.

The exclusivity of Belle Mare Beach extends to the accommodation options, which range from opulent beachfront villas to boutique-style suites. Many of these resorts offer direct access to the beach, ensuring that guests can step out of their rooms and onto the sand within moments.

Infinity pools, private terraces, and outdoor showers are just some of the amenities that elevate the experience. For those seeking a more private escape, some resorts even offer overwater villas, where you can wake up to the sound of the ocean right beneath you. Every detail, from the luxurious linens to the impeccable service, is designed to provide an unparalleled level of comfort and relaxation.

Belle Mare Beach also offers a deeper connection to the local culture and heritage of Mauritius. The nearby village markets provide a glimpse into the daily life of Mauritians, where visitors can purchase handmade crafts, jewelry, and textiles created by local artisans. Traditional music and dance performances are often held on the beach, where guests can witness the island's vibrant culture firsthand. These moments, combined with the luxury of the beach, create a rich and immersive experience that goes beyond the typical resort vacation. It's a place where guests can unwind while also engaging with the unique traditions of Mauritius.

A day spent at Belle Mare wouldn't be complete without a sunset cruise. As the sun begins its descent, the sky transforms into a canvas of warm colors, and the water sparkles under the fading light. Many resorts offer catamaran or yacht cruises at this time, providing a front-row seat to one of nature's most beautiful spectacles. Champagne in hand, guests can toast to a day well spent as they sail along the coast, the gentle motion of the boat adding to the sense of serenity. The sunsets at Belle Mare are nothing short of magical, and they leave a lasting impression on everyone fortunate enough to witness them.

For those traveling with family, Belle Mare Beach is just as welcoming. The calm, shallow waters are ideal for children to splash and play in safely, while many resorts offer kids' clubs with activities tailored to younger guests. These clubs provide everything from treasure hunts to water sports lessons, ensuring that children are entertained throughout the day. Meanwhile, parents can enjoy some much- needed relaxation, knowing that their little ones are in good hands. Family-friendly accommodations, complete with connecting rooms and spacious living areas, make Belle Mare an ideal destination for a luxury family vacation.

Even though Belle Mare Beach exudes luxury, it never feels pretentious. The atmosphere remains laid- back and welcoming, with the natural beauty of the surroundings taking center stage. This balance between opulence and simplicity is what makes Belle Mare so special. Whether you're indulging in a spa treatment, enjoying a gourmet meal, or simply lounging on the beach, the experience is elevated by the stunning environment. There's a sense of timelessness here, where the outside world fades away, and the only things that matter are the sand between your toes and the endless horizon before you.

Belle Mare's appeal lies in its versatility. It's a destination that caters to every type of traveler, from honeymooners seeking romance to solo adventurers looking for a peaceful retreat. The beach's sheer size ensures that there's plenty of space for everyone, whether you want to be in the heart of the action or find a secluded spot to call your own. The freedom to craft your perfect beach vacation is what makes Belle Mare so appealing. Whether you spend your days exploring the ocean or simply relaxing under the sun, Belle Mare offers an experience that is uniquely yours

For nature lovers, Belle Mare Beach provides opportunities to explore beyond the shore. The surrounding area is home to lush nature reserves and botanical gardens, where you can hike, bird- watch, or simply enjoy the beauty of Mauritius' native flora and fauna. The nearby Île aux Cerfs is a popular excursion, offering more pristine beaches and a golf course set against the backdrop of the Indian Ocean. The underwater world is equally captivating, with diving trips to nearby coral reefs offering the chance to see a diverse array of marine life. From turtles to reef sharks, the waters around Belle Mare are teeming with wildlife waiting to be discovered.

In the evenings, Belle Mare Beach transforms into a tranquil haven. The sounds of nature take over, with the gentle rustling of palm trees and the distant crash of waves providing the perfect soundtrack for a quiet night. Many visitors take this time to enjoy a private dinner on the beach, where the soft glow of lanterns and the starry night sky create a romantic atmosphere. Others may choose to relax by the pool, sipping on a cocktail and reflecting on the day's adventures. Whatever you choose, the nights at Belle Mare are just as magical as the days.

Ultimately, Belle Mare Beach is more than just a luxury destination—it's an escape into paradise. The combination of natural beauty, luxurious amenities, and a laid-back atmosphere make it the perfect place to unwind, recharge, and reconnect with the world around you. Whether you're seeking adventure, relaxation, or a little bit of both, Belle Mare Beach offers an experience that is unforgettable. It's a place where memories are made, and where every moment feels like a dream come true.

Chapter 8: The Ecological Wonders of Madagascar's Nosy Be

Nosy Be, an island off the northwest coast of Madagascar, is a beach lover's paradise with a twist – it's also an ecological wonder. The beaches of Nosy Be are breathtaking, with golden sands, swaying palm trees, and the warm waters of the Mozambique Channel lapping at the shore. However, what sets Nosy Be apart is its incredible biodiversity. The island is home to lush rainforests, volcanic lakes, and a rich marine ecosystem, making it a haven for nature enthusiasts. The beaches here are not just places to relax; they are gateways to exploring the island's natural wonders. Visitors can snorkel or dive in the vibrant coral reefs, hike through the dense forests, or simply enjoy the sight of lemurs playing in the treetops. Nosy Be offers a unique blend of beach relaxation and ecological exploration, making it a must-visit destination for those who appreciate both luxury and nature.

Nosy Be, often referred to as the "Perfume Island" due to its fragrant plantations of ylang-ylang, vanilla, and coffee, offers an experience that is as rich in sensory delights as it is in ecological treasures. Walking along its golden shores, you are immediately enveloped in the sweet aroma of its tropical flora, blending with the salty ocean breeze. The beaches here are not just stretches of sand; they are living ecosystems where land meets sea in the most harmonious way. At low tide, the coral reefs reveal themselves, teeming with life. Crabs scurry across the beach, and local fishermen cast their nets, continuing traditions passed down through generations. It's a place where the natural world feels alive, constantly shifting and reshaping with the rhythm of the tides.

The inland parts of Nosy Be are equally enchanting, with rainforests that pulse with the sound of exotic wildlife. Lemurs, Madagascar's iconic primates, swing from tree to tree, their playful antics mesmerizing to anyone lucky enough to spot them. Birds of all kinds chirp in the canopy, and if you're quiet enough, you might catch a glimpse of the rare chameleon changing its colors to blend with its surroundings. For those with a keen interest in botany, Nosy Be offers a treasure trove of endemic plants, many of which are not found anywhere else on earth. The island's volcanic origins have also blessed it with fertile soil, supporting a diverse range of plant life that thrives under the tropical sun.

The marine life surrounding Nosy Be is just as impressive. The waters are home to an array of colorful coral reefs, making it a prime destination for snorkeling and diving enthusiasts. Beneath the waves, the ocean floor is a mosaic of coral gardens, where schools of fish dart in and out of the reef, their scales flashing iridescent colors. Larger creatures also make Nosy Be their home. Whale sharks, the gentle giants of the sea, migrate through these waters, and sighting one of these majestic creatures is a once- in-a-lifetime experience. The island is also a sanctuary for sea turtles, which come ashore to lay their eggs in the soft sand under the cover of night.

One of Nosy Be's hidden gems is its network of volcanic lakes, remnants of the island's volcanic past. These tranquil lakes are surrounded by lush vegetation, creating an almost otherworldly atmosphere. Sacred to the local Sakalava people, these lakes are places of great cultural and spiritual importance.

Visitors can hike to the lakes, where the still waters reflect the surrounding greenery, offering a peaceful retreat from the bustling beaches. The combination of beach and inland adventures makes Nosy Be a perfect destination for those who want to explore the island's diverse ecosystems while still enjoying the comforts of a tropical beach vacation. While Nosy Be's natural beauty is undeniable, it's the warmth of its people that truly elevates the experience. The local Sakalava community is known for its hospitality, and visitors are often welcomed with open arms. Traditional Malagasy music fills the air at night, as locals gather for lively dance performances that tell stories of their ancestors and the natural world around them.

The island's cuisine, a blend of Malagasy, French, and Indian influences, is a culinary adventure in itself. Fresh seafood is a staple, with dishes flavored by the island's abundant spices. Dining on the beach, with the sound of the waves as your backdrop, is an experience that connects you to the rhythms of the island.

The conservation efforts on Nosy Be are also worth noting. Both the local community and international organizations have worked together to preserve the island's delicate ecosystems. Marine reserves have been established to protect the coral reefs from overfishing, and local guides are trained to promote sustainable tourism. The island's rainforests are also under conservation, with reforestation projects underway to ensure that future generations can continue to enjoy Nosy Be's natural beauty. Visitors are encouraged to engage with these efforts, whether by participating in a beach cleanup or by choosing eco-friendly tours and accommodations.

One of the most magical experiences on Nosy Be is the nightly migration of the stars. With minimal light pollution, the island offers some of the best stargazing in the region. As you lay on the beach at night, the sky reveals its secrets, with constellations and shooting stars lighting up the darkness. It's a humbling experience, reminding you of the island's place in the vast expanse of the universe. This connection to the natural world, both seen and unseen, is what makes Nosy Be such a special destination.

For the more adventurous travelers, Nosy Be offers a range of activities that go beyond sunbathing and swimming. Hiking trails wind through the island's interior, offering stunning views of the surrounding ocean and neighboring islands. Guided tours take you to hidden waterfalls, where you can cool off in the crystal-clear pools after a long hike. For those interested in the cultural history of Madagascar, Nosy Be's local villages offer a glimpse into traditional Malagasy life. Here, you can learn about the island's customs, crafts, and the sustainable ways in which the locals interact with their environment.

Nosy Be is not just for the seasoned traveler; it's also a family-friendly destination. The calm, shallow waters of its beaches are perfect for young children to play in, and many resorts offer activities designed specifically for families. Boat trips, dolphin watching, and interactive wildlife experiences provide endless entertainment for children and adults alike.

The island's relaxed pace of life ensures that families can spend quality time together, free from the distractions of the modern world. Watching a sunset with your loved ones as the sky turns from orange to pink is a memory that will stay with you long after you've left the island.

As the day comes to a close, the sunset on Nosy Be is nothing short of spectacular. The sky explodes in a riot of colors, with shades of pink, purple, and orange reflecting off the ocean's surface. It's a moment of pure magic, one that you'll want to capture, but also one that begs you to simply be present and take it all in. As darkness falls, the island's nightlife begins to stir. Beachfront bars and restaurants come alive, offering local rum cocktails and fresh seafood straight from the ocean. The sound of laughter and music fills the air as both locals and visitors celebrate the island's vibrant energy.

Nosy Be is a place where the natural world takes center stage, but it's also a destination where luxury and relaxation are never far away. Whether you're staying in a beachfront villa or a more rustic eco- lodge, the island caters to all types of travelers. The gentle pace of life here allows you to disconnect from the stresses of everyday life and reconnect with yourself, your loved ones, and the natural world. Whether you're swimming with dolphins, hiking through the rainforests, or simply lounging on the beach with a good book, Nosy Be offers an experience that nourishes the soul.

Nosy Be is more than just a beach destination; it's a living, breathing ecosystem that invites you to explore and engage with it on every level. From its vibrant coral reefs to its towering rainforests, the island offers a wealth of natural beauty and biodiversity that is unmatched. But beyond the stunning landscapes, Nosy Be's rich culture and warm hospitality make it a place where you feel like you belong. It's a destination that stays with you long after you've left, calling you back to its golden shores and emerald waters.

Chapter 9: The Untouched Beauty of Sierra Leone's River Number Two Beach

River Number Two Beach, located just outside of Freetown, Sierra Leone, is one of Africa's best-kept

secrets. This beach is the epitome of untouched beauty, with its soft white sands, clear blue waters, and lush greenery that frames the coastline. The beach is managed by the local community, who work hard to maintain its pristine condition and offer visitors a warm welcome. Unlike more commercialized beaches, River Number Two is a place where you can truly disconnect from the world and immerse yourself in nature. The gentle waves are perfect for swimming, and the surrounding hills offer stunning views of the coastline. The local community also provides fresh seafood, making it a great spot to enjoy a meal while soaking in the serene atmosphere. River Number Two Beach is a reminder that some of the most beautiful places on Earth are those that remain untouched by mass tourism, offering a glimpse into the pure, natural beauty of Africa's coastline.

River Number Two Beach, located just outside of Freetown, Sierra Leone, is one of Africa's best-kept secrets. This beach is the epitome of untouched beauty, with its soft white sands, clear blue waters, and lush greenery that frames the coastline. The beach is managed by the local community, who work hard to maintain its pristine condition and offer visitors a warm welcome. Unlike more commercialized beaches, River Number Two is a place where you can truly disconnect from the world and immerse yourself in nature. On a bright morning, the sun casts a golden glow across the beach, creating a breathtaking scene. As the first rays of light touch the sand, the ocean glistens like a field of diamonds. The gentle sound of waves lapping against the shore is a calming soundtrack that soothes the soul. Children play near the water's edge, their laughter mingling with the rhythmic crash of the surf. Local fishermen, in their brightly colored boats, return with the day's catch, bringing with them the promise of fresh seafood for all who visit.

The journey to River Number Two Beach is an adventure in itself. The path leading to the beach is lined with verdant vegetation and towering palm trees. As you walk, you can hear the distant calls of tropical birds and the rustling of leaves in the gentle breeze. The air is filled with the intoxicating scent of saltwater and tropical flowers, creating an ambiance that is both invigorating and tranquil. Once you arrive at the beach, you are greeted by the friendly smiles of the local community. Their hospitality is genuine, and they are eager to share their pride in their beloved beach. They offer guided tours of the area, pointing out hidden spots and sharing stories about the beach's history. You might hear about the old legends that speak of the beach's mystical charm or the tales of how the community came together to preserve this natural wonder.

As the day progresses, the beach becomes a haven for relaxation. Visitors lounge under the shade of palm trees, their feet buried in the cool, soft sand. Some choose to take a dip in the inviting waters, where the temperature is just right for a refreshing swim. The sea is so clear that you can see the colorful marine life beneath the surface, adding to the sense of wonder and discovery. The local community's dedication to maintaining the beach's natural beauty is evident in every detail. They have established eco-friendly practices to ensure that the beach remains unspoiled for future generations. This includes efforts to reduce plastic waste, protect local wildlife, and preserve the surrounding natural habitat. Their commitment is a testament to their deep connection with the land and their desire to share its beauty with the world while safeguarding it.

As evening approaches, the beach transforms into a serene retreat. The setting sun paints the sky with hues of orange, pink, and purple, creating a picturesque backdrop for a quiet evening stroll. The cool breeze that follows provides relief from the day's heat, and the stars begin to twinkle above, adding to the beach's magical atmosphere. Local vendors set up small stalls along the beach, offering delicious, freshly prepared seafood dishes. The aroma of grilled fish and other local delicacies fills the air, tempting visitors to indulge in a culinary treat while enjoying the stunning sunset. Dining on the beach, with the sound of the waves as your accompaniment, is an experience that is both simple and extraordinary.

As night falls, the beach takes on a peaceful silence. The gentle sounds of the ocean continue to provide a soothing backdrop, and the distant glow of Freetown's lights can be seen across the water. It is a time for reflection, for appreciating the untouched beauty of this special place and the efforts of the local community who protect it. River Number Two Beach is more than just a beautiful destination; it is a testament to the wonders that can be found off the beaten path. It stands as a reminder that some of the most captivating places on Earth are those that remain untouched by mass tourism. It offers a rare opportunity to experience the pure, natural beauty of Africa's coastline and to connect with a community that treasures and preserves this pristine paradise.

Chapter 10: The Thriving Marine Life of Egypt's Marsa Alam

Marsa Alam, located on the western shore of Egypt's Red Sea, is a hidden gem for beach lovers and diving enthusiasts alike. The beaches here are a blend of soft sands and crystal-clear waters, set against the backdrop of the arid Egyptian landscape. What makes Marsa Alam truly special is its thriving marine life, making it one of the best diving destinations in the world. The coral reefs are teeming with life, from colorful fish to sea turtles, dolphins, and even the elusive dugong. The warm waters and excellent visibility make it a paradise for snorkelers and divers, who come from all over the world to explore the underwater wonders. On land, the beaches offer a peaceful retreat, with luxury resorts providing all the comforts needed for a relaxing stay. Marsa Alam is a place where the desert meets the sea, offering a unique and unforgettable beach experience.

Marsa Alam, located on the western shore of Egypt's Red Sea, is a hidden gem for beach lovers and diving enthusiasts alike. The beaches here are a blend of soft sands and crystal-clear waters, set against the backdrop of the arid Egyptian landscape. What makes Marsa Alam truly special is its thriving marine life, making it one of the best diving destinations in the world. The coral reefs are teeming with life, from colorful fish to sea turtles, dolphins, and even the elusive dugong. The warm waters and excellent visibility make it a paradise for snorkelers and divers, who come from all over the world to explore the underwater wonders. On land, the beaches offer a peaceful retreat, with luxury resorts providing all the comforts needed for a relaxing stay. Marsa Alam is a place where the desert meets the sea, offering a unique and unforgettable beach experience.

One of the most captivating experiences in Marsa Alam is the chance to witness the incredible diversity of marine life up close. As you dive into the warm, clear waters, you're immediately immersed in a vibrant underwater world. The coral reefs, some of the healthiest and most colorful in the world, create a stunning underwater landscape. Their intricate structures, ranging from delicate branching corals to massive plate corals, provide a habitat for a plethora of marine species. Schools of brightly colored fish dart among the corals, their scales shimmering with every movement. You may encounter parrotfish with their vibrant hues, clownfish darting in and out of anemones, and majestic lionfish with their flowing fins. The sheer abundance and variety of life beneath the surface make every dive a new adventure.

Sea turtles, often seen gliding gracefully through the water, are a highlight of many dives. These ancient mariners, with their gentle demeanor and slow, deliberate movements, are a joy to observe. The sight of a sea turtle slowly making its way through the coral gardens is a reminder of the ancient rhythms of the ocean. Dolphins, known for their playful behavior and intelligence, occasionally make an appearance. Their acrobatic leaps and joyful squeaks bring a sense of wonder and excitement to any diving experience. For those fortunate enough to encounter the dugong, the experience is truly magical. This elusive herbivore, often referred to as a "sea cow," is a rare sight and a testament to the health of the marine environment in Marsa Alam.

The conservation efforts in Marsa Alam are crucial to maintaining the health of these incredible ecosystems. Local organizations work tirelessly to protect the coral reefs and marine life from threats such as pollution and overfishing. These efforts include monitoring reef health, conducting scientific research, and implementing sustainable tourism practices. By educating visitors about the importance of marine conservation and promoting responsible behavior, such as avoiding contact with the coral and refraining from feeding the fish, these organizations help ensure that Marsa Alam's underwater paradise remains pristine.

Back on land, the serene beaches of Marsa Alam offer a stark contrast to the bustling city life found elsewhere. The soft, powdery sands are perfect for lounging and soaking up the sun, while the clear, shallow waters are ideal for a refreshing swim. The beaches are often less crowded than those in more commercialized areas, providing a tranquil setting for relaxation. Luxury resorts, strategically located along the coastline, offer a range of amenities designed to enhance your stay. These resorts feature elegant accommodations, world-class spa treatments, and gourmet dining options. The design of the resorts blends seamlessly with the natural surroundings, providing stunning views of the Red Sea and easy access to the beach.

The local community in Marsa Alam plays a vital role in preserving the area's natural beauty and ensuring that tourism is sustainable. Their commitment to protecting the environment and promoting responsible tourism is evident in their daily practices. Community members are actively involved in conservation projects and work closely with local and international organizations to address environmental challenges. They also play a key role in welcoming visitors and sharing their knowledge of the area. Whether through guided tours or casual conversations, the locals provide valuable insights into the unique characteristics of Marsa Alam and its marine life.

As the sun sets over Marsa Alam, the beach transforms into a magical setting. The sky is painted with vibrant hues of orange, pink, and purple, creating a breathtaking backdrop for a sunset stroll. The cool evening breeze offers a welcome respite from the day's heat, and the tranquil atmosphere invites reflection and relaxation. The night sky, free from light pollution, reveals a stunning display of stars. The clear, dark sky provides a perfect canvas for stargazing, adding to the sense of wonder and serenity that pervades the beach.

Beyond the beach, Marsa Alam offers opportunities for exploration and adventure. Desert safaris provide a chance to experience the stark beauty of the surrounding landscape. The rugged terrain, with its dramatic rock formations and vast stretches of sand, offers a striking contrast to the coastal scenery. These excursions often include traditional Bedouin meals and the chance to learn about the local culture and customs. The combination of desert and sea experiences provides a well-rounded adventure that highlights the diverse beauty of the region.

For history enthusiasts, Marsa Alam's proximity to ancient Egyptian sites adds an intriguing dimension to the visit. Day trips to nearby historical locations, such as Luxor and Aswan, offer a fascinating contrast to the natural beauty of Marsa Alam. These excursions provide insights into Egypt's rich cultural heritage, with visits to iconic landmarks such as the Valley of the Kings and the temples of Karnak and Abu Simbel. The opportunity to explore these ancient wonders adds depth to the overall experience of visiting Marsa Alam.

The hospitality of the local people further enhances the experience. Their warmth and friendliness make visitors feel welcome and at home. Whether sharing stories about the sea or offering recommendations for local attractions, the locals contribute to making Marsa Alam a memorable destination. Their knowledge and passion for their home create a deeper connection to the place and its unique attributes.

In Marsa Alam, the combination of stunning natural beauty, vibrant marine life, and warm hospitality creates a truly unforgettable experience. It is a place where the wonders of the underwater world and the serenity of the desert come together in perfect harmony. For those seeking a unique and immersive beach experience, Marsa Alam offers an unparalleled adventure, leaving visitors with lasting memories of a paradise found.

Chapter 10: The Thriving Marine Life of the Kenyan Coast

The Kenyan coast, stretching from the bustling port city of Mombasa to the serene shores of Lamu, is a region renowned for its vibrant marine ecosystems. This coastline, fringed by a series of stunning coral reefs and sheltered by a series of scenic bays and lagoons, is home to a rich tapestry of marine life. The unique confluence of the Indian Ocean's warm waters and the nutrient-rich upwellings from deeper ocean currents create an environment where marine biodiversity flourishes. The pristine beaches, clear blue waters, and flourishing coral reefs make this region one of the most captivating marine environments in East Africa.

One of the most striking features of Kenya's coast is its extensive coral reef systems. These reefs are among the most diverse and well-preserved in the Indian Ocean, harboring an astonishing array of marine species. The coral formations range from expansive, colorful gardens of branching corals to rugged, rugged reef structures teeming with life. Coral species such as Acropora, Pocillopora, and Montipora form intricate structures that provide essential habitat and shelter for countless marine organisms. The vibrant colors of the corals create a kaleidoscope of hues beneath the surface, offering a visual feast for divers and snorkelers alike.

The marine life supported by these reefs is equally diverse. Reef fish such as parrotfish, surgeonfish, and butterflyfish are commonly seen darting through the coral formations. Parrotfish, with their beak-like mouths, play a crucial role in maintaining the health of the reefs by grazing on algae that can otherwise overtake the corals. Surgeonfish, known for their sharp spines, help to control the populations of algae-eating organisms. Butterflyfish, with their delicate and often striking patterns, add to the vibrant tapestry of reef life. The dynamic interactions between these species create a balanced and thriving ecosystem.

Sea turtles are another prominent feature of Kenya's marine life. The Kenyan coast serves as an important nesting ground for several species, including the endangered green sea turtle and the loggerhead turtle. Nesting sites are found along the beaches of Watamu and Malindi, where female turtles come ashore to lay their eggs. Conservation efforts in these areas focus on protecting these nesting sites from threats such as poaching and habitat destruction. Hatchlings, upon emerging from their nests, face the perilous journey back to the ocean, where they must evade predators and survive the challenges of their early life stages.

Dolphins and whales are frequently spotted along the Kenyan coast, adding an element of excitement and wonder to any marine excursion. Bottlenose dolphins, known for their intelligence and playful behavior, are commonly seen in the coastal waters. They often engage in acrobatic displays and can be observed riding the bow waves of boats. Humpback whales, which migrate through these waters annually, are a spectacular sight. Their massive size and hauntingly beautiful songs contribute to the mystique of Kenya's marine environment. The presence of these cetaceans underscores the health and vitality of the coastal ecosystem.

The Kenyan coast is also known for its rich biodiversity of invertebrates. Sea stars, sea urchins, and sea cucumbers are just a few of the fascinating creatures that inhabit the coral reefs. Sea stars, with their varied shapes and colors, play a role in controlling the populations of other marine organisms, such as coral-eating snails. Sea urchins, with their spiky exoskeletons, graze on algae and contribute to the health of the reef. Sea cucumbers, often overlooked, are essential for the recycling of nutrients within the marine environment. Their presence indicates a balanced and healthy ecosystem.

Mangrove forests, found in estuarine and coastal areas, provide critical habitat for a range of marine species. These unique ecosystems act as nurseries for juvenile fish, including species such as snappers and groupers. The complex root systems of mangroves create sheltered areas where young fish can seek refuge from predators. Additionally, mangroves help to stabilize coastlines and protect against erosion, making them an important component of coastal resilience. The health of mangrove forests is closely linked to the overall well-being of the marine environment.

Seagrass beds, another vital component of Kenya's coastal ecosystems, support a wide range of marine life. These underwater meadows provide food and shelter for species such as dugongs, which feed on the seagrass, and a variety of fish and invertebrates that find refuge among the dense vegetation. Seagrass beds also play a role in stabilizing the seabed and reducing coastal erosion. Conservation efforts are crucial to protecting these delicate habitats from threats such as pollution and coastal development.

The Kenyan coast's marine life is not only of ecological significance but also holds considerable economic value. The health of the coral reefs and associated marine ecosystems supports local fisheries, which provide livelihoods for many coastal communities. Sustainable fishing practices are essential to maintaining the balance of these ecosystems and ensuring the long-term viability of fish populations. Community-based management initiatives aim to involve local stakeholders in conservation efforts and promote practices that support both marine health and economic well-being. Tourism, particularly diving and snorkeling, is another important aspect of the Kenyan coast's marine economy. The region attracts visitors from around the world who come to experience the spectacular underwater world. Diving operators and eco-tourism ventures play a key role in promoting marine conservation by educating visitors about the importance of protecting marine environments and encouraging responsible behavior. The revenue generated from tourism provides funding for conservation programs and supports local communities.

However, the marine ecosystems of Kenya's coast face several challenges. Climate change, pollution, and overfishing are among the major threats impacting the health of the coral reefs and associated marine life. Rising sea temperatures contribute to coral bleaching, which can lead to the degradation of reef structures and loss of biodiversity. Pollution from agricultural runoff and plastic waste poses risks to marine organisms and habitats. Overfishing depletes fish populations and disrupts the balance of marine ecosystems. Addressing these challenges requires concerted efforts from governments, conservation organizations, and local communities.

Efforts to safeguard Kenya's marine life include the establishment of marine protected areas (MPAs) and the implementation of conservation initiatives. MPAs, such as the Watamu Marine National Park and the Kisite-Mpunguti Marine National Park, provide refuge for marine species and help to preserve critical habitats. These protected areas are managed through regulations that aim to reduce human impact and promote sustainable use of marine resources. Education and outreach programs raise awareness about the importance of marine conservation and encourage positive changes in behavior.

Research and monitoring are vital components of marine conservation efforts. Scientists and conservationists conduct studies to better understand the health of coral reefs, track changes in marine biodiversity, and assess the effectiveness of conservation measures. Data collected from these studies inform management decisions and contribute to the development of strategies to address emerging threats. Collaborative research efforts, involving local and international partners, enhance the ability to tackle complex challenges and support effective conservation outcomes.

In conclusion, the thriving marine life of Kenya's coast is a testament to the richness and diversity of its underwater ecosystems. The vibrant coral reefs, diverse fish populations, and essential habitats such as mangroves and seagrass beds are integral to the ecological and economic health of the region. Protecting and preserving these marine environments is crucial for ensuring their continued vitality and the well-being of coastal communities. Through conservation efforts, sustainable practices, and a commitment to addressing the challenges facing marine ecosystems, Kenya's coast can continue to be a source of wonder and inspiration for generations to come.

Summary

Africa's sandy beaches are not just stunning landscapes; they are vibrant ecosystems teeming with marine life and offer a wealth of activities that cater to all interests. This eBook provides a detailed exploration of the continent's diverse beach environments, highlighting their rich marine biodiversity, popular activities, and luxurious accommodations.

1. Kenya's Coastal Riches: The Kenyan coast, stretching from the lively city of Mombasa to the tranquil shores of Lamu, is renowned for its spectacular marine life. Coral reefs along this coastline support a dazzling array of species, including parrotfish, butterflyfish, and the occasional sighting of sea turtles and dolphins. Activities such as snorkeling and scuba diving offer unparalleled opportunities to explore these underwater treasures. Luxury resorts in areas like Diani Beach and Malindi provide high-end accommodations with easy access to these marine wonders, making them ideal for both relaxation and adventure.

2. Mozambique's Hidden Paradises: Mozambique's coastline is dotted with pristine beaches and rich marine environments. In places like Tofo Beach and the Bazaruto Archipelago, visitors can experience some of the best diving in Africa. The coral reefs here are home to a variety of marine life, including whale sharks and manta rays. Fishing enthusiasts will appreciate the opportunities for deep-sea fishing, where they can catch species such as marlin and tuna. Coastal lodges and resorts offer a range of accommodations, from rustic charm to luxury, ensuring a memorable stay amidst Mozambique's natural beauty.

3. Tanzania's Jewel: Zanzibar, an island off the coast of Tanzania, is famous for its crystal-clear waters and vibrant marine life. The coral reefs around Zanzibar and Pemba Island are home to an array of tropical fish, sea turtles, and occasionally, playful

dolphins. Snorkeling and diving excursions are popular activities, with numerous operators offering guided tours. Zanzibar's hotels and resorts, ranging from beachfront bungalows to opulent five-star properties, provide luxurious amenities and stunning ocean views, making it a perfect destination for both relaxation and exploration.

4. Seychelles' Tropical Wonders: The Seychelles, with its idyllic beaches and turquoise waters, is a paradise for marine enthusiasts. The coral reefs around the main islands, including Mahé, Praslin, and La Digue, are rich in biodiversity, featuring colorful fish, sea turtles, and even occasional shark sightings. The clear waters are ideal for snorkeling and diving, while the beaches offer opportunities for relaxing or engaging in water sports. Luxurious resorts and boutique hotels on the islands offer world-class amenities, including private beach access and gourmet dining.

5. South Africa's Coastal Charms: South Africa's beaches, such as those in Cape Town and the Eastern Cape, are renowned for their dramatic scenery and diverse marine life. Cape Town's beaches, including Clifton and Camps Bay, provide spectacular views and opportunities for spotting marine life like seals and whales. The Eastern Cape, known for its more remote and tranquil beaches, offers excellent whale watching and snorkeling experiences. Coastal hotels and lodges cater to all preferences, from chic urban retreats to serene seaside escapes

1. Egypt's Underwater Wonders: Marsa Alam, located on the Red Sea, is celebrated for its thriving marine life and stunning coral reefs. Divers and snorkelers flock to the area to experience the rich biodiversity, including colorful fish, sea turtles, and the rare dugong. The warm waters and excellent visibility make it a prime location for underwater activities. High-end resorts along the coast provide luxurious accommodations and direct access to the reef, ensuring guests can fully enjoy the marine environment.

2. Senegal's Coastal Beauty: Senegal's coastline, particularly around Dakar and the Petite Côte, offers a unique blend of sandy beaches and rich marine life. The waters here are home to a variety of fish species, and fishing is a popular local activity. Tourists can enjoy snorkeling and diving in the clear waters, with opportunities to see vibrant coral reefs and diverse marine life. Coastal hotels and lodges offer a range of accommodations, from comfortable guesthouses to upscale resorts.

3. Gambia's Serene Shores: The beaches of The Gambia, especially around Banjul and Kololi, are known for their serene beauty and rich marine life. The clear, calm waters are ideal for snorkeling and swimming, with opportunities to spot fish and occasionally dolphins. The Gambia's coastal accommodations range from budget-friendly lodgings to luxurious resorts, providing comfortable stays with easy access to the beach.

4. Sierra Leone's Untouched Treasures: Sierra Leone's River Number Two Beach, with its pristine sands and clear waters, is a hidden gem. The beach is managed by the local community, ensuring its natural beauty is preserved. The marine life here includes colorful fish and occasionally sea turtles. Visitors can enjoy peaceful swimming and relaxing beach walks. Local lodges and guesthouses offer a chance to experience the area's hospitality while enjoying the tranquil environment.

5. Namibia's Desert Meets Sea: Although less known for its marine life, Namibia's coastline, particularly around Swakopmund and Walvis Bay, offers a unique experience where the desert meets the sea. The cold Atlantic waters are home to marine species such as seals and various fish. Activities include boat tours to see seals and dolphin watching. Coastal hotels in Swakopmund provide a blend of comfort and adventure, reflecting the region's unique landscape.

This eBook captures the essence of Africa's sandy beaches, highlighting their diverse marine life and the wide range of activities available. Whether you are a nature enthusiast, an adventure seeker, or simply looking to relax, Africa's coastline offers something for everyone, with luxurious accommodations ensuring a memorable stay.

About the Author

Leonard Kisau is a distinguished scholar and researcher with a deep passion for exploring and documenting the natural wonders of Africa. With extensive expertise in academic research and writing, Leonard has dedicated his career to studying and sharing insights on various subjects, including marine life and environmental conservation.

His work spans multiple disciplines, reflecting his commitment to understanding and preserving the diverse ecosystems of the African continent. Leonard's extensive travels and research have provided him with a unique perspective on Africa's coastal environments, allowing him to craft engaging and informative narratives that highlight the region's natural beauty and ecological significance.

Don't miss out!

Visit the website below and you can sign up to receive emails whenever LEONARD KISAU publishes a new book. There's no charge and no obligation.

https://books2read.com/r/B-A-KLGKC-XCYYE

Connecting independent readers to independent writers.

Cartoons have a magical way of taking us on wild adventures, sparking our imaginations, and filling our days with laughter and wonder. For children, they are more than just animated characters on a screen — they become friends, teachers, and heroes in a world where anything is possible. Cartoons & Me is a journey into this enchanting realm, where imagination knows no limits.

In this book, we explore how cartoons shape young minds, nurture creativity, and offer life lessons wrapped in vibrant colors and playful stories. Whether it's learning about teamwork, courage, or simply having fun, cartoons play an important role in children's development. This eBook is designed to celebrate the joy and magic that cartoons bring to

---

1. https://books2read.com/u/3JBydB

2. https://books2read.com/u/3JBydB

our lives, while offering insight into their impact on children's emotional and cognitive growth.

Join us as we dive into this world of animated wonders, where every page holds a new adventure, a lesson to be learned, and endless fun!

Read more at https://www.familymedia.com.

About the Author

Leonard Kisau is a devoted husband, father of four daughters, and a passionate writer who draws inspiration from his personal experiences to share stories that resonate with parents and families.

Read more at https://www.familymedia.com.